*There is no such thing
as someone else's children.*

Glennon Doyle

A *Child* PROPHET

CHARLES P. BUSCH
Founder / Fields of Peace

A

Child

PROPHET

Lately, I have been listening for a voice. Perhaps you have been listening too. Someone who can lead us through the threats which now darken our world and the future of our children. We all know the list:

Seas rising, deserts expanding

Leaders threatening nuclear strikes

Genocides

Famines

Pandemics

War upon war

100 million refugees migrating over borders, mountains, seas.

These catastrophes threaten our existence. And planet. To meet them will require an unprecedented cooperation between nations. No one nation can meet them alone. We will have to grow up fast. For so long peace has been seen as the pastime of dreamers. Now, it is the most practical business of all. And the most urgent.

A *Child* PROPHET

There are many voices asking to be heard—commentators, pundits, podcasters, politicians, scholars, preachers, authors. Some are wise, many are helpful. But among them I rarely hear what I listen for, an authority that comes from beyond the self.

There are poets who qualify. Who, like children, say what they see. Who hear what the wind says to the leaf, and the leaf answers back. Who report the dark thing that waits just below the horizon. Poet Kim Stafford writes:

Whereas the world is a house on fire;
Whereas the nations are filled with shouting;
Whereas hope seems small, sometimes
a single bird on a wire
left by migrations behind.
Whereas kindness is seldom in the news
and peace an abstraction
while war is real . . .

But poetry requires listeners, and ours is not a nation that looks to poetry. It is thought to be difficult, and incidental in the order of things. What's needed is a voice that is unavoidable.

I think of the ancient Hebrew prophets who walked the streets of Jerusalem. Who shouted. Accosted. Who would not go away. They called their nation's reliance on armed might "evil." And militarism "idolatry." They said God is on the side of the gentle, the humble, the contrite. Not the aggressive. They promised that peace among nations would come.

They shall beat their swords into plowshares,
and their spears into pruning hooks;
nation shall not lift up sword against nation,
neither shall they learn war anymore.

- Isaiah

I know the days of prophets are thought to be long over. But surely, with life on earth threatened with extinction, there is a voice to be heard. Rising up. Calling out. A prophet in our midst.

Recently, I read a news story about a 5-year-old boy caught in the Ukraine war. His name is Arthur. He and his mother, Miranda, lived in the city of Mariupol. Seeking safety from the invading Russian soldiers and nightly bombings, they found a ruin and hid in the basement. It was dark and cold. There were rats. But they did not dare step out. Their daily ration was a cup of water each and half a cookie. They knew it was night when the bombing began.

For two months they endured this darkness. Then, little Arthur began to scream. He could not stop. On and on for two days and nights he screamed. Seeing he was close to dying, Miranda put him on her back and ran into the night. She ran through the smoke, shouts, fires, the shaking earth. Somehow they found safety. But today, Miranda says, Arthur no longer speaks. No longer smiles. He has fallen silent.

Arthur did not scream for his mother's attention. She was holding him. She was as helpless as he was. He may have hoped for someone outside to hear and

rescue them. But I believe he screamed to be heard beyond Mariupol, beyond the bombs, the nightmare. Children know when something has gone terribly wrong. When our sense of kinship is gone. Arthur screamed to be heard by humanity. Failing that, he became silent.

Arthur's silence accuses us all. Sickens us all. But in that silence there is a gift. I heard it first as a commotion of voices: The cries of children caught in war. Children in Ukraine, in Gaza, Israel, Sudan, the Congo. And as I listened, those cries became one cry, one voice. One message:

I am your child. Stop war. Now.

Perhaps you hear it too. The whisper. The repetition. The plea.

I am your child. Stop war. Now.

A *Child*
PROPHET

In modern warfare, for every 1 combatant killed, 9 civilians are killed, the majority of them children. This has been true for decades. *War has become the killing of children*. How perfect that the prophet sent to us is a child.

Children know nothing of history or politics or poised missiles. But they know intuitively that all is connected. That to touch a leaf or stone or hand is to thrill or trouble all that is.

They wonder how we have forgotten this. Wherever children go, whatever school or gathering they enter, they ask: *Will I make a friend*? They know how to construct a safe world. Friend-by-friend-by-friend. In the voice of Janna, a young Palestinian girl, poet Naomi Shihab Nye writes:

We are made of bone and flesh and story
but they poke their big guns
into our faces
and our front doors
and our living rooms
as if we are vapor.
Why can't they see
how beautiful we are?

The saddest part?
We all could have had
twice as many friends.

A *Child* PROPHET

Prophets speak to nations and individuals alike. They name the failing, the particular injustice we have allowed to grow large and is about to be our undoing. They demand change. They tell us it is not yet too late. They say in the streets what the voice of conscience has been saying to us all along.

To kill a child is an absolute wrong
War has become the killing of children.
You must not be a part of war. Any war.

Our world is on the brink. The forces of death gather. Apocalyptic movies multiply. Birth rates drop. Armies line the borders. The cooperation necessary to save ourselves requires peace among nations. Peace, the most practical business of all. And the most urgent. For this, a prophet has been sent to us. A child prophet, saying,

I am your child. Stop war. Now.

How will this change happen? Through you and me. I know no other way. How do we to begin? Surely there are many ways. The way I know is through the power of the spoken word. Words are inherently creative. Spoken, they can heal, bring rain, part seas, move mountains. They can also awaken hearts and move nations.

The words I say out loud each morning are simple. They are words that make a promise.

I will not be a part of the killing
of any child,
no matter how lofty the reason.
Not my neighbor's child
not my child,
not the enemy's child.
Not by bomb, not by bullet,
not by looking the other way.
I will be the power that is peace.

Saying these words each morning changes me. Perhaps they will change you. My fears are eased. The peace I want to feel, comes. And I see that each child caught in war is like my son, Gabriel. Beautiful. Precious. And so alive. Each with a mother who prays every time her child goes out the door. Each with a father who feels helpless to protect his child from the indifference, cruelty, fires of the world. I see that the child caught in war is my child.

To the ancient Hebrew prophets, the taking of a single life was as momentous as the taking of ten thousand lives, and the saving of a single life as momentous as the saving of ten thousand lives. How perfect that the prophet sent to us is a child, saying,

I am your child. Stop War. Now.

Voice of the Child

By Reem Ghunaim, Executive Director, Fields of Peace

Charles reminds us that the prophet sent to us is a child. Every day at Fields of Peace, we listen for that child's voice. It comes from classrooms and playgrounds, from refugee camps and mountain towns. It comes from Oregon and from Palestine, and soon, from every corner of the world. It asks us the same question Arthur's silence asks: *Will you hear me?*

Fields of Peace began with a moral declaration: *Stop the killing of children*. That call remains our foundation. Over time, our mission has grown to meet the depth of that truth; to not only condemn violence but to build the conditions for peace. Today, our purpose is clear and urgent: **to cultivate a global peace movement inspired and led by children.**

Through our Generation Peace Program, Fields of Peace creates a diplomatic stage for children; a place where they can act as our young diplomats, replacing bombs with friendships and borders with bridges. Beginning with connections between students in Oregon and Palestine, we are building a model of *citizen diplomacy* rooted in empathy, storytelling, and shared humanity. They become citizen diplomats who learn that to touch a friend across the world is to touch the future itself.

In these exchanges, a sacred reversal occurs: adults learn from children. Their instinct for friendship cuts through the walls of politics. Their drawings and poems remind us that empathy is an intelligence the world has neglected. Their courage, rooted in curiosity and guided by wonder, shows us that leadership begins in the heart. In a world ruled by calculated minds, they remind us what it truly means to lead with love.

Each time a child says *I am your child. Stop war. Now.*, we are called to act. To listen more deeply. To protect every life as our own. To build a world where no child must scream to be heard. This is the work of Fields of Peace; awakening the prophet within every child, and within each of us who still believes in the boundless power of love.

Voice of the Child

The work of peace belongs to all of us. Whether through teaching, mentoring, giving, or simply listening, every act of compassion brings us closer to a world where every child can live surrounded by love. At **Fields of Peace**, we believe true transformation begins by harnessing the power of presence; by choosing to see every child as our own and nurturing the strength, imagination, and hope that already live within them.

We invite you to join us in creating a world that loves its children; a world that listens, understands, and acts with empathy and courage. Together, through friendship, storytelling, and shared action, we can build the foundations of lasting peace.

Visit **fieldsofpeace.org** to learn more about the *Generation Peace Program* and how you can be part of this growing movement that echoes the children's call:

I am your child. Stop war. Now.

Thanks / Credit

Design, Layout, & Production
Tim Gilman, timmyroland.com

Editing
Cathey Busch, Rod de Luca, Frances Menlove

Poetry - by permission of authors
Naomi Shihab Nye & Kim Stafford

The Tiny Journalist, Poems, by Naomi Shihab Nye, BOA Editions, Ltd, Rochester, NY, 2019, pp 21, 22

A Proclamation for Peace, Translated into World Languages, by Kim Stafford, 2024

Scripture
Isaiah 2:4

Resource
The Prophets, by Rabbi Abraham J. Heschel, 1st Perennial Classics, 2001

Board Members

Harry Anastasiou / Oregon
Lydia Asana Ngua / Florida
Charles Busch Founder / Oregon
Ryan Gallagher Chair / Hawaii
Bior Garang / Kenya
Cameron Hansen / Oregon
Melissa Madensk i/ Oregon
Wayne Martin / Oregon
Martha Payne, Treasure / Oregon
Annabelle Schwartz, Secretary / New York

Artist in Residence

William Kucha
Painter, Sculptor, Singer, Songwriter

Advisory Board

Suman Aggarwal, PhD
Founder & President,
Shanti Sahyog Center for Nonviolence, India

Rod de Luca
Former Chair of Fields of Peace Board

Alex del Vecchio
Peace Village Committee

Patrick Hiller, PhD
Director, War Prevention Initiative

James Owaka
Center for Nonviolence, Africa

Kim Stafford
former Poet Laureat of Oregon

David Swanson
Founder & Director, World Beyond War

Afterword

When I was 13, my family moved to New York City so my father could go to graduate school. We arrived on a Sunday in August. I remember my thrill at seeing the famous skyline as we crossed the George Washington Bridge. Our home was Howells, Nebraska, population 706. We knew we were hicks.

My mother, father, older sister and I spent that first day walking the streets of mid-town Manhattan—Times Square, Fifth Avenue, Tiffany's, Rockefeller Center. "Look, Look," was all we could think to say.

I remember, as we waited for a light to change, noticing a man on the corner across from us. His arms were outstretched, and he was shouting something. When the light changed and we started toward him, I saw he was old, and his suit shabby and too big on him. In each hand he held out a thin tract. "Take one, Take one," he said. My heart raced as I hurried past. *What a scarecrow,* I thought. *What a way to end up.*

Today, I smile at that memory. Now I am the old man with a message to save the world, the fool with a tract in each hand saying, "Take one, Take one."

I could not have guessed I would end like this, nor enjoy it so much.

Fields of Peace
Generation Peace

Cultivating a global peace movement
inspired and led by children

Fields of Peace

Post Office Box 2,
Lincoln City, Oregon 97367

fieldsofpeace.org

www.ingramcontent.com/pod-product-compliance
Lightning Source LLC
Chambersburg PA
CBHW052118020426

42335CB00021B/2823